Where Have You Be

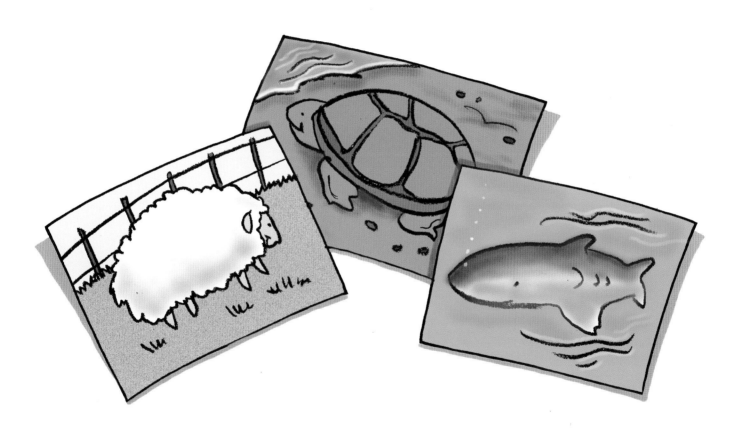

Have you been to the zoo?

2

Yes!
We saw zebras and giraffes.

3

Have you been to the farm?

Yes! We saw some sheep and pigs.
They were in pens.

5

Where have you been?
Have you been to the aquarium?

6

Yes, we have. We saw fish.
They were in big tanks.

Have you been to the museum?

Yes, we have.
We saw big dinosaurs.

Have you been to the nature center?

Yes! We saw ducks and turtles.

11

We saw big bugs and snakes.

We saw trees and flowers
at the nature center.

Have you been to the park?

Yes! We saw birds and squirrels.
They were in the trees.

We were on the swings!